BOOK ANALYSIS

By Cassandra Gibbons

My Brilliant Friend

BY ELENA FERRANTE

Bright
≡Summaries.com

ELENA FERRANTE

ITALIAN NOVELIST

- **Born in Naples in 1943.**
- **Notable works:**
  - *Troubling Love* (1992), novel
  - *The Lost Daughter* (2006), novel
  - *The Story of the Lost Child* (2014), final novel of the Neapolitan series

Elena Ferrante is an Italian novelist who was born in Naples, southern Italy, in 1943. She writes under a pseudonym and hides her true identity. Attempts to unmask her have been criticised in the literary world as an invasion of privacy. It has been theorised that she is actually a man using a female pseudonym; an idea that she has derided and claimed comes from the sexist belief that women are not good writers. She gives interviews to the press by email and through a translator.

Ferrante rose to international fame with the publication of her Neapolitan series, which comprises four novels and begins with *My Brilliant*

Friend. Ferrante has stated in interviews that she considers the four novels to be one work that had to be published serially because of its immense length. She has hinted in interviews that at least parts of the novels are autobiographical in nature, which is heavily suggested by the fact that the protagonist, Elena Greco, shares her first name with the author herself. Ferrante worked on the Italian-American television adaptation of *My Brilliant Friend.*

MY BRILLIANT FRIEND

A BILDUNGSROMAN

- **Genre:** bildungsroman (a coming of age story)
- **Reference edition:** Ferrante, E. (2015) *My Brilliant Friend*. New York: Europa Editions.
- **1ˢᵗ edition:** 2012
- **Themes:** friendship, violence, class, love, education, Italian society in the mid-20th century

My Brilliant Friend is the first in the four-part Neapolitan series of novels by Elena Ferrante. The novel follows two bright young girls, Elena Greco and Lila Cerullo, as they navigate their childhood and teenage years in post-war Italy. The novel is written in the first person from the perspective of Elena. It is divided into three sections: Prologue, Childhood and Adolescence. *My Brilliant Friend* includes an Index of Characters, a useful key for the reader to refer back to in order to keep track of a novel so densely populated with characters.

The novel has received critical acclaim and been adapted into a stage production, as well as the 2018 Italian-American television adaptation. The novel has been translated into many languages; the English translation is by Ann Goldstein. It has sold over ten million copies in 40 countries. It has been lauded as a brilliant example of women writing about female friendship, and Ferrante has been described as one of the best novelists of our time by a reviewer for *The New York Times*.

SUMMARY

A RETURN TO CHILDHOOD

In Turin, Elena, a woman in her sixties, receives a phone call from her old friend's son, Rino. He is calling to tell her that his mother, Lila, has been missing for two weeks. Elena is not surprised, having been told long ago by Lila that she wanted to disappear without a trace. Elena tells Rino to search his mother's room. He comes back to her to report that his mother has taken all of her possessions with her. Elena tells Rino not to call her again, and decides, in some anger, to write down all the details of her and Lila's story.

Elena is drawn to Lila in primary school despite Lila's poor behaviour. They start playing next to each other in the street without talking, and eventually become close friends. One day when they are playing they swap dolls, and Lila throws Elena's doll Tina down the grate and into the cellar of the building they are next to. Elena throws Lila's doll down in retaliation. They look for their dolls in the cellar but cannot find them, so Lila concludes that they must have been taken by Don Achille Carracci, a feared figure in the neighbourhood. Carracci is so feared that Elena and Lila hesitate to beat Carracci's son Alfonso in an academic competition, fearing repercussions for their families. When Lila does beat him, his older brother Stefano rages at Lila, grabbing her tongue out of her mouth.

The whole neighbourhood is stricken with violence and death. The state of medicine at the time meant that children could die from sepsis if they suffered a simple cut, such as the one Lila sustains after another boy she beats in school, Enzo, throws a rock at her forehead. The husband of Melina Cappuccio is murdered, and the family is aided by Donato Sarratore, a railway worker. Melina falls in love with Donato and begins a rivalry with his wife Lidia that drives the Sarratores out of the neighbourhood. The eldest child, Nino, professes his love for Elena, but she tells him that she cannot promise herself to him, though she returns his feelings.

Lila convinces Elena to confront Don Achille about their missing dolls, despite his reputation as a monster. He denies taking them, but gives them money to buy replacements. Lila uses the money to buy a novel, *Little Women,* which the two girls avidly read. Their intelligence is remarked upon and praised by their teacher, Maestra Oliviero, who goes to each of their families with the aim of getting permission for the girls to go to middle school. After some initial hesitation, Elena's parents allow her to continue her education, but Lila's father Fernando is adamant that his daughter is finished with school. When she protests, he throws her out of the window, breaking her arm. Elena successfully passes the test to get into middle school, which causes a rift between her and Lila. Meanwhile, Don Achille is murdered and the girls' friend Carmela Peluso's father is arrested.

EARLY ADOLESCENCE

Elena and Lila spend less and less time together as Elena goes to school while Lila works in her father's shop (after one year at a vocational school), but they continue to compete with each other. Lila takes books out of the library, reading voraciously and studying the subjects Elena covers at school like Latin and Greek. Elena initially struggles at school, but succeeds when she applies herself and, notably, when Lila gives her study tips. Lila clearly struggles with jealously over the fact that Elena is being educated while she is working in a shop. She is often brusque with Elena for this very reason. Lila and her brother, Rino, design and hand-make a pair of men's travelling shoes, which enrages their father.

As the girls hit puberty and develop, they begin to increasingly receive attention from the boys in the neighbourhood. Elena matures first, and in her eternal quest to beat Lila, says yes to the first boy who asks her to be his girlfriend even though she does not particularly like him. Lila is slower to develop than Elena, but when she finally reaches puberty, her graceful beauty draws the attention of many boys and even a few men. Lila lets Pasquale Peluso, Carmela's brother, down gently when he declares his feelings for her. But when Marcello Solara, who Lila had previously threatened with a knife after he tried to drag Elena into his car, tells Lila he has serious intentions, Lila tells him that she considers him to be an animal and would never become engaged to him. Her father angrily urges her to reconsider, not wanting to get on the wrong side of the Solaras, who are a powerful family in the neighbourhood with notorious connections.

A rivalry between two factions, the Solaras on one side and Lila, Elena and their friends on the other side, culminates in a competition to see which side can set off the most fireworks on New Year's Eve. Rino in particular is obsessed with beating the Solaras, and enlists the help of Stefano Carracci to do so. This heals some rifts in the community, as Pasquale and Carmela Peluso reconcile with the Carraccis (Signor Peluso is in jail for the murder of Don Achille). Pasquale, Rino, Enzo and Stefano are all particularly defensive of Lila, who is attracting a lot of male attention not just from Marcello but from other men too. When the Solaras are defeated in the battle of fireworks, they begin shooting at their opponents. Lila experiences a feeling of disassociation that she describes as an "episode of dissolving margins" (p. 89). Lila is adamant that she is not going to marry Marcello Solara, but she finds it difficult to persuade her family to let her enact her will as they see a marriage between the two as very beneficial, regardless of Lila's feelings. Marcello often dines with the Cerullos and expresses an interest in buying the shoes that Lila and Rino made, an idea Lila refuses to countenance.

Meanwhile, Elena is allowed to go to Ischia for the summer and stay with the cousin of Maestra Oliviero, Nella. She swims, practices her English with Nella's guests and writes to Lila frequently. When the English family leave, the Sarratores replace them, and Elena is overjoyed at the prospect of seeing Nino, with whom she has not spoken in years despite the fact that they go to the same high school. Elena finds Donato pleasant company, and is surprised when Nino tells her that he is a hypocrite who betrays his mother constantly. Elena is happy when Nino kisses her but less so when he shows an interest in Lila, and she is devastated when he leaves the following day. She receives a letter from Lila on her birthday and is struck by two things: firstly, despite her lack of formal education Lila writes much better than Elena does, and secondly, Lila is struggling to keep Marcello Solara at bay. Elena considers going home to help her friend but does not really want to leave. That night, Donato kisses her and gropes her. Elena freezes during the assault and is disgusted, both with him and with herself for feeling some pleasure. The next morning she leaves a note for Nella and returns to Naples.

TWO DIVERGING PATHS

Elena returns to Naples to find that Lila has been spending time with Stefano Carracci, who buys the shoes she made and invests in her father's business. She accepts his proposal of marriage and tells Marcello, who threatens to kill her and Stefano. Elena goes back to school and is humiliated to realise that she needs glasses. When they break she gives them to Lila and Stefano pays for the repairs. Stefano and Lila begin to spend money without a care, which causes tensions between them and their less wealthy peers. Whenever Elena mentions something she has learned at school, Lila steers the conversation back to whatever Stefano has bought her recently. When Marcello Solara spreads rumours that Lila performed oral sex on him, Stefano, instead of resorting to the usual violence in order to defend his fiancée's honour, agrees with Lila that they should rise above such pettiness.

Enzo, Pasquale and Antonio are outraged that Stefano and Rino are willing to let Marcello say horrible things about Lila without reprisal, and set the Solara brothers' car on fire. This is despite the fact that a jealous Pasquale calls Lila a whore for selling herself to Stefano Carracci, which causes Enzo to threaten him. Lila has to deal with her future mother-in-law, Maria, and future sister-in-law, Pinuccia, constantly undermining her. She enlists Elena's help in dealing with them. Elena, meanwhile, begins to feel left behind as the wedding preparations get underway, and accepts Antonio's offer of a relationship even though she loves Nino. When Donato returns looking for Elena, she gets Antonio to threaten him and force him to leave the neighbourhood.

Elena is dragged into the wedding preparations, as she is able to successfully negotiate between Lila and her future in-laws. Elena gets into trouble at school by arguing with the priest during a lesson, but she is praised by Nino and Professor Galiani, a communist teacher. Nino encourages her to write about the exchange for a small publication he sometimes writes for. When he reads the article, which Lila edited, he is disappointed to learn that Elena writes better than he does. Enraged, Elena asks Antonio to pick her up because she knows Nino will be watching. Elena knows that she should break up with Antonio because she does not love him, but resolves to wait until after the wedding. Lila is beginning to suffer from pre-wedding nerves, particularly after her attempts to invite Maestra Oliviero are rebuffed. Elena helps her to dress on the day and Lila wonders if things will turn out well for her.

The wedding turns out to be a grand social event; the guests dress in their absolute finest. Elena worries about Lila, but is comforted by the decisiveness with which she says her vows. Elena begins to feel out of place amongst her friends, a feeling which is compounded by her mother's disapproval of her relationship with Antonio, whom she considers to be beneath her daughter. At the restaurant reception following the service, Elena sits with Nino and Marisa Sarratore and Alfonso Carracci rather than Antonio, Enzo, Carmela and Pasquale. Nino tells her that there was not room in the publication for her article and she has to swallow her disappointment. Lila is shocked to see the Solara brothers arrive at the reception when she expressly forbade them from coming. Her horror is compounded when she sees that Marcello is wearing the shoes that she and Rino made and sold to Stefano. The novel ends as she turns as white as her dress in shock, anger and betrayal.

CHARACTER STUDY

ELENA GRECO

Elena Greco, sometimes known as Lenuccia or Lenù, is an intelligent but unconfident girl who lives in Naples with her parents and three siblings. Her father is affectionate with her but she has a strained relationship with her mother, who resents all the money that is spent on Elena's education. Despite their occasional hostility, Elena's parents support her education. Elena is a dedicated student and is also kind and caring: she is trusted to babysit the stationer's children and is allowed to go to Ischia and earn her keep by working in Nella's guest house.

The novel is written in the first person from Elena's perspective as she, in her sixties, looks back to her childhood and retells it with the express purpose of writing it down (whether Elena in her adulthood has the intention of creating a novel from this transcription is unclear). The narrative voice, is therefore blessed with the benefit of hindsight, and the older Elena can dissect her younger self's actions and understand her motivations better than anyone. It is clear that Elena, in her childhood, is motivated by her desire to keep up with her friend Lila. She is panicked to be slightly less academically gifted than her friend, and then, when she has reached the heights of academia and overtaken Lila, she becomes obsessed with attaining Lila's levels of beauty and the attention paid to her by men and boys alike. Elena is characterised by her good nature, her loyalty and her lack of self-confidence.

RAFFAELLA 'LILA' CERULLO

Lila Cerullo is an extraordinarily gifted girl who teaches herself to read at the age of six. Her academic brilliance is stymied by her father's unwillingness to pay for the education of a girl, which he sees as pointless. Lila's mother is more sympathetic but ultimately sides with her father. Lila is close to her brother, Rino, who wants her to be educated and to be able to choose who she marries. Lila's home life is chaotic and sometimes violent, including one instance when her father throws her out of the window for arguing with him about going to school. Unable to go to school, Lila continues to study of her own volition taking out countless library books using membership cards for herself, her mother, her father and her brother Rino. In this way, she is able to take out four times as many books.

Lila is characterised not only by her intelligence and strong will, but also by her ambition. When her education comes to an end, she feels like she has to give up on her dream of writing novels for a living. She instead focuses all of her attention on manufacturing shoes, hoping to expand her father's shoe repair business into a shoe production line. Her father is unappreciative of her ideas, instead wanting her to simply marry a convenient man – in this case, Marcello Solara – and become a housewife. In order to escape the attentions of Marcello Solara, whom she despises, Lila instead begins a relationship with Stefano Carracci. She sees marriage as her only opportunity to have some freedom and to take care of her family. It is unclear if she actually loves Stefano, although she says that she does. Her personality is enigmatic; even Elena often cannot tell what she is really thinking.

MAESTRA OLIVIERO

Maestra Oliviero is the primary school teacher who nurtures the intelligence of both Elena and Lila. She lobbies both girls' parents to let them continue their education but is unable to persuade the Cerullos. She seemingly washes her hands of Lila when this happens, considering her to be a lost cause and urging Elena to drop her as a friend. She is a snob who introduces the concept of 'plebs' to Elena, encouraging her to get herself out of the neighbourhood. Her actions drive the plot forward, particularly in relation to Elena; Maestra Oliviero not only successfully convinces her parents to allow her to continue school, but also arranges for Elena to go to Ischia for the summer, where she encounters the Sarratores.

STEFANO CARRACCI

Stefano Carracci is the son of the feared Don Achille, who is murdered in the 'Childhood' section of the novel. He grows up to become a successful businessman, running the grocery store with his mother, Maria, and two siblings, Pinuccia and Alfonso. He is driven by a desire to make money, and also by a will to maintain his status. He is combative and competitive when it comes to the battle of the fireworks on New Year's Eve because he wants to assert himself over the Solaras, the dominant force in the neighbourhood. However, his desire to make money supersedes this rivalry, as can be seen when he sells the shoes that Lila made to Marcello despite the trouble he knows it will cause in his marriage. Although he claims to love Lila, there is also the possibility that to him she represents just another status symbol as the most desired woman in the community.

DONATO SARRATORE

Donato Sarratore is a railway worker-cum-poet who is forced to leave the neighbourhood when the attention he pays the widow Melina turns into a violent rivalry between her and Donato's wife, Lidia. Donato is admired by Elena, which he takes advantage of by groping her and telling her that he loves her. Donato's son, Nino, despises him for his infidelities and tries to spend as little time with him as possible. Donato uses poetry to seduce women, and seemingly feels little or no guilt towards his loyal wife. His desire for attention and adoration compels him to betray her for his own gratification.

MARCELLO SOLARA

Marcello Solara is the son of Silvio Solara, who owns a bar in the neighbourhood and has Camorrist connections. Marcello and his brother Michele are violent, corrupt thugs who go around the neighbourhood in their car, dragging girls into the back seat at a whim. Marcello tries to drag Elena into his car and is threatened with a knife by Lila. Far from enraging him, her forthright behaviour captivates him, and he spends the rest of the novel in hopeless pursuit of her. He showers her family with chocolates and even a television set in the hope of winning her affections. When she turns him down he threatens to kill her and her fiancé, but is unable to do so, he claims, because of how much he loves her. Nonetheless, his rejection causes him to seek revenge against her, and so he buys the shoes she and Rino so carefully laboured over, and wears them to her wedding, to which he was explicitly not invited.

ANALYSIS

FEMALE FRIENDSHIP

The central theme of the novel is friendship, specifically that of Elena and Lila. While they belong to the same circle of friends, their relationship is much closer and even inspires envy in some people (like Nino) who wish they had that sort of connection with a friend. The eponymous friend of the novel's title at first appears to be Lila: as she is extremely intelligent, and the novel is written in the first person from Elena's perspective, that would make Lila 'my brilliant friend'. It is in fact Lila who refers to Elena as "my brilliant friend" (p. 312), although the moniker could arguably be applied to both. The word 'brilliant' can have a double meaning. On the one hand, it can signify great talent or ingenuity, which it does; on the other hand, it can mean that the friend in question is particularly loyal and steadfast. The Italian word from which 'brilliant' is translated, 'geniale', means brilliant in the sense of intelligence, and so does not have this double meaning.

The friendship between Elena and Lila is defined by its competitiveness. The girls are suspicious and wary of the possibility that their friend may outdo them. As the novel is narrated from Elena's perspective, this most frequently manifests itself in her worries that Lila is smarter, prettier and wilier than her, but in fact it is Lila who truly has something to be jealous about regarding Elena: her education. Elena is motivated to succeed in her education largely because she wants to catch up with and eclipse Lila's natural ability. She sometimes takes for granted that she is lucky to be receiving a formal education at all, something that Lila will never experience. Lila projects an image of self-confidence but is deeply insecure about her lack of education, which she tries to remedy by educating herself. She can only take her studies so far without formal instruction, however, and so is denied many of the opportunities Elena enjoys. She tries to pretend that her lack of education bothers her less than it does by embracing her other opportunities, namely producing hand-made shoes and marrying Stefano.

The disparity in the girls' respective educations puts a strain on their friendship. Lila's jealousy of

Elena's education breeds resentment, while Elena is taken aback by Lila's often brusque and sometimes cruel dismissals of her studies. This is a coping mechanism for Lila, which the older Elena can understand, but the young Elena is often taken aback and even hurt by this attitude. The fact that the girls put themselves in competition with one another is a barrier to their friendship, because each secretly hopes that the other will not do well. This portrayal of female friendship is honest if brutal, as it conveys the ways in which girls and women are pitted against each other and taught not to root for and support each other but to revel in the failure of others and take their defeats as victories.

SEXISM IN 1950S ITALIAN SOCIETY

The representations of sexism in Italian society in the 1950s are manifested in two distinct areas: education and honour. While Fernando Cerullo refuses to pay for an education for Lila or for Rino, he strongly implies that were he to educate one of them, it would most certainly be Rino because of his sex:

> "'School? Why, did I go to school?' [said Fernando]. 'No.' [replied Rino]. 'Did you go to school?' 'No.' 'Then why should your sister, who is a girl, go to school?'." (p. 69)

Elena's parents relent and allow her to continue her education, but feel uneasy about it. Elena's mother in particular resents the money her daughter's education costs that could be spent on other things, and she is quite possibly also jealous that her daughter is receiving opportunities that were denied to her. The limited career opportunities for women in Italy in the 1950s and 1960s undoubtedly weigh heavily on the minds of Elena's parents: even if Elena excels, which she does, the likelihood of her having a career seems small.

Lila, on the other hand, is expected to make a fortuitous marriage in the absence of her education. Her father hopes to persuade her to marry Marcello Solara because a connection like that could elevate the entire family. Lila is a pawn that he uses to his own advantage, and he reacts with violence and rage when Lila tells him that she does not want to marry Marcello. Lila is so pressured to marry a man she despises that her only way out is to marry another man she prefers, which turns out to be Stefano. The Cerullos even save up to pay Stefano a small dowry; this reinforces the idea that the marriage is a transaction of goods rather than a partnership of equals. Lila is treated as a commodity, as if she has no agency at all.

The notion of a dowry links in with the concept of 'honour'. A woman is considered to have honour if she eschews sex outside of marriage. Her own free will has little to do with it, however: a raped or sexually assaulted woman, like Ada Cappuccio, who is dragged into the Solaras' car, is considered to have lost her honour even if she bears no responsibility for the actions of her assailant. The restoration of a fallen (i.e. sexually active or raped) woman's honour is traditionally achieved through violence: either the woman herself is killed, normally by her male relatives, or the man who took her honour (whether consensually or by force) is killed or at least attacked. The men in *My Brilliant Friend* generally choose the latter option, restoring their female relatives' honour by beating up the man who has dishonoured her. This is linked to the concept of a dowry because dishonour affects the amount of money given to the future husband, which again reinforces the idea that women are commodities to be sold and traded by men. A dishonoured woman would typically be accompanied by a larger dowry, as she would be considered 'damaged goods'.

There are numerous examples of men in the novel using violence to defend or restore the honour of women. For example, when Marcello Solara spreads rumours that Lila performed oral sex on him, Pasquale, Enzo and Antonio set the Solaras' car on fire and arrange for them to be beaten up (it is unclear if the men themselves carry out the attack). This is despite the fact that Lila's preferred course of action, which is followed by Rino and Stefano, is to rise above the petty gossip and not dignify it with a response. Pasquale in particular is incensed by Rino's willingness to avoid a violent confrontation to restore Lila's honour. This is despite the fact that Lila's life and reputation are no concern of Pasquale's, as she has turned him down as a potential partner. Pasquale feels responsibility for Lila's actions despite her express wish that he does not interfere with her life and that no violence be committed in her name. His entitlement to her, as a possession, is unmistakeable.

CLASS

The third predominant theme of the novel is undoubtedly class. The wealth, or lack thereof, of various characters completely changes how they are treated and how they interact with the world around them. Class also intersects with other characteristics, like sex. For example, Marisa Sarratore belongs to a family who can afford holidays to Ischia and so, despite her lack of academic brilliance, is educated. Her parents educate her knowing that she will likely become a secretary and then a housewife, and will not put her academic studies to much use. On the other hand, Lila, who is far more brilliant than Marisa, is not allowed to go to middle school and high school because she is female and because she comes from a poor background. The lack of education afforded to poorer students then of course limits social mobility. Lila has to marry a businessman, to whom she is ill suited, in order to raise her social standing. When she embraces her fiancé's money, she is castigated by her friends, who consider her to be a snob who has sold herself. Sexism intermingles with these feelings, particularly when Pasquale calls her a whore. Despite the legitimacy of her marriage and her professed feelings for Stefano, her attempts at carving out a better life for herself and her family are undermined and she is attacked. Her hard work in the shoe shop goes largely uncredited and she is denounced as little more than a prostitute.

Elena, on the other hand, is afforded an education and with it the possibility of upward social mobility. She is conflicted in her privilege, and feels unable to make the most of her social advantages without abandoning her family and her roots. She feels the divide keenly when her friends who come from a similarly poor background, such as Pasquale, Rino, Antonio, Enzo, Lila and Carmela, make fun of middle class people on their trips into Naples. By the wedding, Elena is feeling faintly embarrassed by her friends' uncouth behaviour and their raucous actions.

> "It was during the journey to Via Orazio that I began to be made unhappy by my own alienness. I had grown up with those boys, I considered their behaviour normal, their violent language was mine. But for six years now I had also been following daily a path that they were completely ignorant of and in the end I had confronted it brilliantly." (p. 69)

Elena ends up spending much of the wedding reception talking to Nino and ignoring her boyfriend, Antonio, who has made an effort to please her by buying a suit for the wedding. She wonders whether she should have taken Maestra Oliviero's advice and dropped Lila as a friend. The novel ends as Elena asks herself what she truly wants out of life: someone like Antonio or someone like Nino; a marriage like Lila's or a university education; to stay in the neighbourhood in which she grew up or to escape it. Her answers to all these questions are also bound up in her inability to value herself as an entity separate from Lila.

FURTHER REFLECTION

SOME QUESTIONS TO THINK ABOUT...

- In your opinion, is Lila a good friend to Elena, and vice versa? Justify your answer.
- The subheading of the 'Adolescence' section is 'The Story of the Shoes'. Discuss the role the shoes play in the novel and what they represent for Lila.
- Discuss the representation of violence in the novel.
- Having read *My Brilliant Friend*, discuss the ways in which you think female friendship may differ from male friendship or mixed sex friendship.
- Why do you think Ferrante begins her novel in the present day and writes the bulk of the novel as a flashback? What are the strengths/weaknesses of this approach?
- In your opinion, to whom does the title of the novel refer? Justify your answer.
- In what way, if any, is *My Brilliant Friend* an Italian novel?
- Discuss the reasons why Elena Ferrante might want to write under a pseudonym.

We want to hear from you!
Leave a comment on your online library
and share your favourite books on social media!

FURTHER READING

REFERENCE EDITION

- Ferrante, E. (2015) *My Brilliant Friend*. New York: Europa Editions.

ADAPTATIONS

- *My Brilliant Friend*. (2018) [TV series]. Saverio Costanzo. Dir. Italy/USA: Wild Side/Fandango/Umedia.

www.brightsummaries.com

Ebook EAN: 9782808019286

Paperback EAN: 9782808019293

Legal Deposit: D/2019/12603/131

Cover: © Primento

Digital conception by Primento, the digital partner of
publishers.